Descent

POEMS

Descent

Kathryn Stripling Byer

Louisiana State University Press ꓫꓫ Baton Rouge

Published by Louisiana State University Press
Copyright © 2012 by Kathryn Stripling Byer
All rights reserved
Manufactured in the United States of America
LSU PRESS PAPERBACK ORIGINAL
FIRST PRINTING

DESIGNER: *Mandy McDonald Scallan*
TYPEFACE: *Filosofina*
PRINTER AND BINDER: *IBT Global*

Library of Congress Cataloging-in-Publication Data
Byer, Kathryn Stripling.
 Descent : poems / Kathryn Stripling Byer.
  p. cm.
 "LSU Press Paperback Original."
 ISBN 978-0-8071-4750-4 (pbk. : alk. paper) — ISBN 978-0-8071-4751-1 (pdf) — ISBN 978-0-8071-4752-8
(epub) — ISBN 978-0-8071-4753-5 (mobi)
 I. Title.
 PS3569.T6965D47 2012
 811'.54—dc23

                                                                                                    2011051748

The paper in this book meets the guidelines for permanence and durability of the Committee on Production Guide-
lines for Book Longevity of the Council on Library Resources. ∞

The author would like to thank the following journals and resources in which these poems have appeared:

Callaloo ("Confederate Flag" issue): "Southern Fictions"; *Cave Wall:* "Lost"; *Crab Orchard Review:* "What I See Now";
Connotations Press: An Online Artifact: "Over"; *North Carolina Conversations:* "Retablo" (in an earlier version); *The
Cortland Review:* "At the End," "My Grandfather's Cattle Gap," and "Shadow Sister"; *The Georgia Review:* "Easter
Afternoon"; *Heartstone:* "Last Light"; *North Carolina Literary Review:* "Drought Days"; *Shenandoah:* "Blackberry Road"
and "Gone Again"; *The Store of Joys* (North Carolina Museum of Art): "Gone" (originally "June Pastoral"); *storySouth:*
"Nightfishing" and "Big Tease"; *Western North Carolina Woman:* "Take this, she said . . ." (from "Drought Days").

Aretha's Hat: Inauguration Day 2009 (chapbook): "First Presbyterian," "Gladiolas," "Outside," and "Some Rock Re-
members"; *American Life in Poetry:* "I don't know . . ." (from "Southern Fictions"); the North Carolina Library As-
sociation: "Beginning at the Bottom."

My gratitude to Jacar Press, Durham, North Carolina, for its letterpress, limited edition publication of *Southern Fic-
tions* in Spring 2011.

For my father
C. M. Stripling (1920-2006)

Contents

Descent

Morning Train

I'm going home on the morning train . . .
—PRECIOUS BRYANT, GEORGIA BLUES SINGER

So long, so long, the train sang
deep in the piney woods, well out of sight.
As sound only, it found me
where I spread my fingers for eggs in the straw
and pretended I could not hear somebody calling
a name I did not want to answer to,
long vowel reaching for nobody I knew as yet,

sounding an emptiness
deeper than I thought could blow through
the cracks of this song where I'm kindling a fire
for my fingers to reach toward,
a kindling that transforms whatever it touches
to pure sound, a pearl, say,
that's cupped in my palm

like a kernel my teeth cannot crack,
the pulse of it strung note by note round my neck,
that old rhythm-and-blues beat
I can't stop from singing me home
on this slow morning train
of a poem, its voice calling
downwind, *What took you so long?*

PART I

Soon we will descend the widow's descent in the memory fields
and raise our tent to the final winds: blow for the poem to live, and blow
on the poem's road.
—from "Here the Birds' Journey Ends," Mahmoud Darwish
Translated by Fady Joudah

At the End

he said nothing of sun rising
over the hoar-frosted scrub pines

and nothing of mist he saw rising
from deer scat. Never a word

did he whisper of morning cold burning
his throat as he stood at the dawn's edge.

His open mouth bore but a fleck
of blood, last uttered syllable

as he fell back to the pillow,
ice growing lace shutters over

his eyeballs, but not before he pushed
through holly-thorn into the clearing,

the deer turning toward him,
a rush of quail lifting their wings

as he watched his breath leaving
like white cloth he once saw

a carnival magician unwind from his mouth
and throw to the crowd where he stood

wanting proof but ashamed to raise
his hands like the other boys, grabbing at air.

for Ulmont Campbell, my grandfather

5

Retablo

She gathered her children
around the casket wherein
lay my grandfather.
There in the Slumber Room

of the whites-only funeral
home, she prayed
for each child he'd fathered,
including the one laid

away long before I was
born. I did not witness this.
I avoid open caskets. But now
with a few strokes of language

I must make the lid
of the coffin come unstuck
to show me his sales-rack
gray suit. His feet

laced in Sunday black
shoes. His mouth
from which no snore
escapes. His forevermore

closed eyes, first thing
she'd fancied about him the day
he came calling to fetch
a stray dog. *Bird's egg blue*

she remembered, first thing,
or so I've been told, that begins
to decay once the coffin lid's shut
and we've all turned away.

Gone

Long before I could read Lorca
I wanted to give myself over to green
as he had and be lost like a sleepwalker
in it. I wanted to hide in the honeysuckle

and never come home if it meant I must stay
by the telephone, waiting for someone
to call with the doctor's pronouncement,
my mother then turning to us saying
over and over again in my memory, *Gone*.

Such a word I would never repeat
to the oaks that held sway round my favorite pasture,
or blackberry bushes I dreamed would stay
unscythed by road crews sent forth to claim
right of way. *Verde, que te quiero verde*,
I'd gladly have cried if I could,
but where are such beautiful words

when we need them? And what if that's all
this poem means now I'm middle-aged: words
as a way to want green back again
and myself in the throes of it,
even though I've learned enough about Lorca
at last to be quite sure that no *verde*
anywhere spending its June on this earth
could have outstayed for one blessed
second what waits at the end
of the line, always some bloodless voice
trying hard to sound human across so much
distance, its words still escaping me.

Down

When the telephone rang,
I was brushing my hair
in the bathroom and squinting
my eyes just enough
so my face in the mirror
looked almost like those
on the covers of *Seventeen*,
distant and dreamy,
the dogwoods and
pear trees in flower,
the windows wide open,
my mother's voice suddenly
crying out, *gone*,
almost gone, and the door
slamming after my father,
whom I can still see driving
too fast, as always,
down that sandy road
to the house where my uncle
lay dying, my mother
forgetting to turn off
the oven as she grabbed
the keys to our Chevrolet,
flinging back one last
command, which I tried
to obey, standing there
at the edge of the known
world, my hands holding on
to the fence stretched
alongside the highway,
while I watched the swollen
sun that I knew nobody,
not even Jesus, could
talk into not going down.

My Grandfather's Cattle Gap

frightened me. Cattle knew better
than to cross, but my cousins did not
and took turns fording slats
over hardly more depth than a ditch.
I refused to play Russian Roulette
on what felt like a train trestle over

a bottomless pit. Blame that story
my mother had told me:
the tomboy whose leg fell through,
broken, of course, and the train
chuffing closer and closer.
The cattle gap rattled like coffin slats.
What if some poor heifer dared
to cross over? Her bones splintered
each time I thought of it. Poor cow,
she would be shot before dawn.

Poor granddaughter, she would be
rushed to the hospital,
destined to hobble through summer
on crutches. Yes, I blame my mother
for that silly fear. Not to mention her dream
in which the cattle gap rattles again and again
as she drives toward the burning house
where everyone she loves lies sleeping.

Drought Days

For my grandmother, Carrie Mae Campbell

1.

Rain, because prayed for,
was always called God's answer,
God being what gave
or withheld whatever we needed.

A merciful god, and we'd smell dirt beginning
to dampen. But judgment? Then He in the sky
would become in my nostrils the odor
of earth at its most unforgiving.

God stank like a singed field.
His taste in my mouth like a rusty nail.

I wanted him kept well away
from the places I loved,
his narrowed eyes raking the world.

2.

The sky must have shone back a message
on drought days, the way
she'd look into it over and over

to see if a cloud might be forming,
and inside that cloud a small storm seed
of hope from the heaven side.

*Let's pretend we could walk through
the mirror. What would we find on the other
side?* She never liked that game,

it went against God's design,
and too much like walking into her own dark
as if through the eye of a hurricane.

To enter the kingdom,
she'd stand in the kitchen and look
out the window at what He

had wrought, corn that sang when
the wind came, a husband who shoveled hay
into the cow pen, the empty yard waiting

for the child growing inside her: her life
seeming suddenly all mass,
and her knees almost too weak to bear it.

3.

Every shining surface seemed mirror.
The shaft of a carving knife.
Kettle-shank polished to clarity.
Windows that framed her by day
and at night by the oil lamp
revealed her as lost in a ghost forest.
Suddenly she'd set to work
righting lopsided hair ribbons.
A lapsed curl.

Even the yard that she walked upon
served as a backdrop for shadow
while she flounced her skirt like a jonquil.

Or playing at age,
humped her back like a guinea hen,
clucking her way toward the garden,
grown old in a trice.

Was this vanity?
To look on what she had been given
and see herself everywhere in it?

4.

After supper she roamed to the highway
to watch how the sun swelled,
a hot-air balloon,
or else threatened to melt like a butter-pat

after which heat began loosening its tourniquet.
Then came the jays back, the grass-singers
piping up. Then came the moon over pitch pines.
Came wind and the screech owl.

She ducked into woods
where the sun seen through
pine needles wavered
like wild fire when she winced.

Just one spark.
That's all she ever wanted.

5.

At the moment of death he'd hear
rain, he joked.
Drought over. The pond
rising. Flint River cresting to record
heights. Heat lightning

banging its anvil. Sparks
flying. Rain thumping tin
like the school marm's rebuke
she knew he'd not forgotten.
The ruler's pop. Three times.

Swarmed by the dust he stirred,
he clenched his fists
round the tractor's wheel.
He ground his teeth
on the grit of his field.

6.

Now take this, she'd say, her mouth
full of pins—a bird's tail
of fastenings held tight
against revelation. What now?
And where? I was lost
till she lifted the limp tape

and held my hand hard on
the selvage while she reckoned
grain-line and measurement.
Taking the straight of it
so that the garment would fall
clean to plumb. What she called a good

finish. A clean sweep to hem-level,
a dress in which she could walk out the front door
or be laid down at last like the lady she knew she was.

7.

To measure the cloth needed,
she'd hold each bolt against our flesh,

folding the crisp panels over
by arm's length till she had her estimate.

She could spend hours stroking broadcloth
and dimity, mulling the question of how much

of what and for whom while we watched
our identity come down to color and texture.

Which of us orange-flowered broadcloth
that shone like her kitchen linoleum,

which the cerulean-blue-dotted swiss
(marked to half-price) that tickled her palm

or the lavender crepe de Chine
sliding through fingers that soothed it?

8.

With feathers she had plucked herself,
she stuffed two pillows
for my marriage bed and crocheted

with silver hook a chain of white lace
to stitch round the edges of two pillowcases.
Soon her fingers could not thread

a needle, nor hold fork or spoon.
By then her man was gone,
wrapped tight inside a dream of trees

that leafed out every spring: time
to plow, time to seed, time to bury
yet again what he had sown.

(I wonder, do the trees commiserate
about the leaves they let go,
all the loosenings they must live with?)

If I could, I'd stitch a Double Wedding Ring
against the morning when they woke to sun
stuck, days on end, to every window pane.

9.

When the pond dried up,
my cousins and I filled oil drums
with my grandfather's hoses

and pulled on our bathing suits,
climbed in like daughters of lawyers
or bankers and stood there pretending

we dawdled at Myrtle Beach
or Sanibel Island. The clouds passing over
might that very morning

have darkened the boardwalk
in Panama City. Her white Leghorns scratched
in the sand. His pigs wallowed.

The water began to smell
rusty, more tractor oil to it
than tropical coconut. We hauled

ourselves out, feeling
silly and shriveled, our skin flecked
with rust, knowing we were still stuck

on the farm. We would always be
hicks. Pink and flabby like pickled
pig flesh in our grandmother's jars.

Soul food, I grew up to hear it called,
as if the collards and side meat
we set on our table had been sanctified

but by stories we knew were not ours,
in which we were no more than
bystanders, and not always innocent ones.

Outside

If I imagine a narcissus outgrowing its sheath,
I must also imagine a girl with my name
lying cold on the bed, having outgrown her life.
Outside, those flowers pushed up through the sod

while she labored to push her breath into the room
where her mother sat, wiping her face.
Maybe she dreamed a kite she held
lifted her into the sky. Maybe
she let go and fell into
darkness. I cannot imagine the darkness

her mother fell into. I'd rather imagine
her father outside with his shotgun,
aiming his grief at the sky.
Or a squirrel. A stray chicken.
The mule he could not spare to grief. I imagine
him pulling the trigger again and again
to block sounds from the sickroom. Not hard to imagine
he could not look into his daughter's eyes,
blank as the sky he could not blast with shot.

I will not let him go back inside. I will
keep every door locked. Every shade drawn.
No telephone, yet, to be answered,
but I take it off the hook anyway,
mouthpiece that never stops wanting more:
What happened? What happened? Tell me.

Lost

for Kathryn Campbell, 1916–1928

1. Dirt Road

She stood in the ruts of it,
waiting while he drove his pickup
through infinite aisles of pecan trees
till finally she shucked her sandals
and pointed her big toe
to scrawl S.O.S. in the sand,

for a crop duster might any moment fly
over, and he, the old father she loved,
might be startled out of his lassitude
and call out her name
as he'd croon to his cattle at day's end,
sack full of oats in his arms.

Never mind the old woman
who stood at the gate calling, closer
than she liked to think about
home being, dark bedrooms scented with camphor
and bacon grease. Tick-tock of ancestral
clock on the mantel. Dust of her mother's
talc settling. The mirror that held her
while she watched her hair being brushed
till it crackled. No, she was not meant

to smile back at herself in its ugly embrace,
just as she was not meant to be left
on this dirt road for darkness to take her
as it took the pasture on either side,
turning its clover to green slime on pond water
through which her father's cows came
trolling toward her like giant
fishes lifting their heads from the water.

2. Sleep

Outside the farm lay in moon haze
she fancied was snow, though she'd never
seen snow nor expected to see it,
for South was her point on the compass,
her elders said, no need to wander,
what for? Wasn't this moon

she'd wakened to good enough?
Weren't these trees singing with quite enough
locusts as anywhere? Wouldn't she soon see
how light on the sand masked an unyielding
surface, hard as cement from the broom straw
of four generations and litters of hound dogs
whose bodies slept under the shade trees?

What would she do with snow anyway,
after the first thrill,
but wait for the earth to show through
again, soggy and yielding?
Snow could kill livestock, crack a tree's
branches. Make a girl want to die,
that was the gist of it, she supposed,

giving herself up to sleep that came just
as she noticed how quickly the moon had gone
down behind her father's pecan trees,
turning the snow that had wakened her
back into home ground, the lay of
what she knew would be hers
someday, the dark of it stretching for acres.

3. Haunt

She bargains with death,
saying let me spend
one more night in the bed
where my mother enfolds me,
her already turning to ghost girl,
her first heartbreak

still beating. Let me wake up
one more morning to
hogs squabbling
over the corncobs my father
throws, mules
begging hay and the shiftless
hounds already searching
for shade. Let me

count all my fingers
and toes, run my tongue across
teeth, feel my stomach
begin to know hunger again.
Let my feet feel the floor.
Let me walk in my cotton shift
into the last thing that ever
I'll ask: Let me open

my mouth,
knowing this is my end
of the bargain, this yearning
to say *Here I am*
but am not.

PART II

I inherited a dark wood . . .
—from "Madrigal," Tomas Tranströmer

Southern Fictions

> . . . human kind
> Cannot bear very much reality.
> —FROM "BURNT NORTON," T. S. ELIOT

1.

My father drapes his battle flag across
a back-room window. If I tried to tell
him why I wish he wouldn't, I'd have hell
to pay. Or else I'd end up sounding crass
and smug. It's just not worth it. Let it pass.
I squelch my fury at this flag and all
it means, the stubbornness, the pride, the gall
of my own people trying hard to pass
the buck, as if what happened never did
exactly, or even if it did, it doesn't mean
what "they" think: something awful—racist swill
and all that liberal junk. I know the truth hid
out those days in silence, but, what does it mean,
this flag? Refusal to admit our guilt?

2.

I don't know. I still can't get it right,
the way those dirt roads cut across the flats
and led to shacks where hounds and muddy shoats
skulked roundabouts. Describing it sounds trite
as hell, the good old South I love to hate.
The truth? What's that? How should I know?
I stayed inside too much. I learned to boast
of stupid things. I kept my ears shut tight,
as we kept doors locked, windows locked,
the curtains drawn. Now I know why.
The dark could hide things from us. Dark could see
while we could not. Sometimes those dirt roads shocked
me, where they ended up: I watched a dog die
in the ditch. The man who shot him winked at me.

3.

While good ole boys lit out with baseball bats,
I dawdled in the bathroom staring at my face
a long time in the mirror. Saw no trace
of beauty there, so counted zits. Sighed. That
was that. Another self-examination, the last
of that day, as it turned out. My father's place
was empty at the table. My mother paced
the kitchen, and we worried until half past
when we heard his pickup churning over ruts.
He slammed the door too hard. He walked too slow.
We watched him mouthing words we couldn't hear.
When he came in, he said *Nobody had the guts*
to say go home. He shook his head and told how
those boys with their bats had bullied blacks clear

to the county line, yelling don't come back
again. My father drove home, in his head
the words he might have said. *They aren't bad*
boys, he told us. *Just misguided. The right tack*
to have taken would be fatherlike and ask
them if they knew what they had done. Instead
he'd not said anything. He picked at bread
set out for sandwiches. The black
girl come to clean house stood outside
calling, *Here I am.* We pitched our voices low
and changed the subject. Cleared the table, let
her in. My father sat there for the longest time
still brooding. That was forty years ago.
I wait. This story isn't finished yet.

4.

She never knew what hit her, the last words
or the first, and in between, the story.
Round and round it went. The school bus slowly
trembling to a stop. The little girl who never heard
her mama screaming as the crimson sports
car sped around the bus and knocked her forty
feet. Did not slow down and sped from sight. *A sorry
spectacle,* my father said. It never once occurred
to me that men would lie about what
happened. There had been not one but
twenty witnesses. Mostly children, mostly black
of course. They didn't count. In court
the lawyers for the bleached blonde got
her off. She wasn't speeding. We can ask

the witness who had seen it all himself.
The white man in his trailer truck who drove
up as the red car disappeared, observed
the scene and then proceeded to absolve
his neighbor's wife of blame. He'd tailed
her all the way, never once had she gone
over thirty-five. How could she kill
that child? He saw her slowing down.
Who killed her then? Nobody knew.
Must have been some other car. Another blonde.
In half an hour, the jury thought so too.
(I can't deny it's safer to stay blind.)
What else to do? *She's damn lucky,* said
my father, *it's not my child she left dead.*

5.

When the feminist poet flew down from New York,
I drove her to campus, an hour's
easy drive. We chatted all the way there,
mostly politics. I liked her so much I shored
up my courage and told her the work
those boys had done, the macho way they
bragged, how no one had the nerve to say
shut up. She misinterpreted my words,
assuming I had suffered in the midst
of bigotry, silently doing my very best
to row against the tide. It sounded so good
I kept quiet, ashamed to say I'd been no activist.
That I'd done nothing, joined no protests,
felt no guilt. Had seen no reason why I should.

6.

However poor we are, we aren't black,
said a neighbor. That was bedrock, solid ground,
the core of our identity. The one unyielding fact
of life. As long as we had *them* around,
we had someone to look down on and that
was hard to come by those days when the sound
of insults on the newscasts made what
we'd become to outside eyes come clear: clods
from the bottom of the backwoods.
Does my voice shake when I read my verse
outside the South, for fear I seem a dunce
or worse? Yes, I'm ashamed to say. I've stood
beside some famous poets and wished my words
could sound as if I came from somewhere else.

Gone Again

I used to believe Scarlett would forever be
    standing atop that small rise of Georgia clay
    staring at Tara, intoning *Tomorrow, Tomorrow,*
        that sad pace of syllables, the Old South
newly colorized, ready to hoodwink another generation
        of belles. But I won't be among them,
no doddering old lady still telling of how
        I remember my mother reciting her tales
of the premiere at Loew's Grand Theater,
    all Atlanta agape at the glitterati. No ma'am,

I have sat through that gorgeous monstrosity
        five times in English and once in dubbed
Spanish. Miss Scarlett does not anymore stir
        me into a passion of Southernness.

Once I imagined myself limping home
        with a worthless mule, nothing but rags
in a wagon, waiting for the moon to reveal
        the house still standing, me weeping
into my muddy hands, having survived
        such a journey and all for a lost cause.

I didn't much like Scarlett after the war.
        Standing there in the moonlight
was our shining moment, unfazed by
        the real sounds of hound dogs
        and katydids, down on the road
a horn playing "Dixie," its drunk driver heading
        back home to his fraternity house.
        So frankly, my dear,

I don't give a damn whether or not Scarlett's
    barbecue ball gown looks brand new
        after sixty-two years. Scarlett makes me feel

tired—all those hours I wasted, enraptured
   by someone whose skin was sheer
celluloid, whose voice, when the reel came
   loose, gibbered like mine when I tried
to pretend I lived just down the road
   from that movie set, cotton fields painted
   on canvas, the loyal slaves hoisting
     up sacks full of nothing
    but chaff for the wind, that old
Hollywood hack, to keep blowing away.

Shadow Sister

Sometimes I still see you
haunting the thickets around every
stubble field. You swing the rusty gate open,
then you swing it shut. In the after-dust
you scrawl your hopscotch and dare me
to leap over cow pies and cockle burrs.

Trapped in your eyes I see Sherman
march through here all over again.
I see smoke rising out of the cornfields
while you, having only a poor piece of dishcloth
to beat against those flames,
keep stamping them out with your bare feet.

No wonder you love to say
you are Miss Scarlett right down
to the bone, when you aren't being Orchid
or Jasmine from way back,
a belle who loves picking her way
through a wasteland of snake-nettle.

Sometimes I still want what you want,
the keys to a red-hot convertible,
top down, and who the hell cares
if a hard rain comes,
we're headed north, east,
west, we are out of here, girl.

But it's too late.
I see what you are. A long drought,
the kind I have known more
than one farmer's daughter to curse,
shake her fist at,
for all the good that ever does her.

Gladiolas

Or glads, as we called them,
their spikes shooting up every summer
in my grandmother's garden.
Finally a wife with a small plot
of ground, I planted my own,
pushed the tubers down
deep. Wiped my hands on my jeans.
Waited two months. They bloomed.

Bending over their folds of magenta
and scarlet, I raked my left cornea
over the stub left behind by my scissors.
I stood with bouquet in arms, *Oh,*
this means nothing, nothing at all,
but the world had become blurred
and stayed that way. One week. Another,
until I was forced to admit I could not change

this other world no longer sharpened
by edges. It floated like what lies
beneath a pond's surface. It shimmered.
The skin of my eye had been sheared
by the wound of a cut blossom,
liquid of Lorca's doomed *verde.*
No help but to let the eye doctor
scrape off the crud of that old skin
and let the new grow back again.

Aren't you glad, my eye blinked,
once the bandage came off,
that again you can see how
the stamens hang quivering,
the hand reaching out for the stalk?

What I See Now

I see yucca and winter stubble along
their route, now and then markers
noting the sites where they camped,
singing hymns, keeping watch as the Ancient
Ones do in the Bibles they carried.

I take note of hay bales like those
I grew up seeing everywhere,
Billy's Tire Center crumbling to nothing
beside a small graveyard with plastic blooms
bled now to white from the weather.

Montgomery waits straight ahead,
looking these days like anyplace else
with its Wal-Mart and Home Depot.
Driving through downtown,
we tick off the fast-food chains.
Why not MacDonald's? We order

our coffee to go. Senior
discount: the girl at the register
rings it up, looking no older than
seventeen, her story holding
not much left of what happened

here
forty years ago.
Blue eyes,
I notice. Stark
purple eye shadow.

❧

My best friend at *Finishing School*,
as we called it while lifting
our lily-white pinkies
and pursing our lips for effect,
came from Selma,
a beauty queen born late
to parents who asked that their only child
not room with anyone whose shade
of iris bloomed darker than blue.

Smoking cigarettes, bold in the parking lot,
we watched a regiment of frat men
in Rebel duds raising the Bonnie Blue Flag
while their girlfriends stood swaying
in hoop skirts: a squadron of cheerleaders
urging them onward, their brave drunks,
defenders of white Southern womanhood.

Meanwhile her mother was driving
across the state line with a black woman
kept in the back seat to mind
many layers of pink lace and satin,
arriving in time for the ball gown
to be lifted out and ironed ever so carefully
down in the basement where

those not invited to Mayday
Ball, rapt as an ashram
of wannabe's, inhaled
our Salems right down
to the filter and exhaled
our smoke rings,
observing them hang
in the singed air like ghosts
before fading away.

Spanish moss hung,
my friend later told me,
from phony live oaks round the dance floor
while black waiters served phony champagne,
no alcohol within a fifty-mile radius lest
we be banished, forevermore losing
our chance to be "finished"
like fine crystal ready to be rung

by just the right finger.
My friend's gown came back
splashed with whiskey, a stain
that could never be washed from its pink
satin bodice. My friend did not come back
the next year. She transferred to Birmingham
Southern. I wonder what she saw

with those bonnie eyes when the 16th Street
Baptist Church blew, and the little girls pulled
from the rubble lay finished
beyond comprehension,
their role in this story I see now
as being a stubble field at the edge

of an altered state
line I'm still
trying to cross
with an old
roadmap wrinkled
as yesterday's
pink satin
inside my skull.

PART III

I inherited a dark wood, but today I am walking in the other wood, the light one.
—from "Madgrial," Tomas Tranströmer

They flew to the fourth world
    below.
   Down there
was another kind of daylight.
—from *Ceremony*, Leslie Marmon Silko

Over

For my father

When Kelly flew over
the farm with your ashes,
the field waited,
October light keen
as a ploughman's blade
slicing through sod.

When Kelly's plane rose
over loblollies,
trailing its message-
smoke, we knew
you'd settled yourself
into alfalfa stubble,
eternally comfortable
inside the dirt
you had tilled.

What a helluva way
to come home,
Daddy. Oh
you knew all along
what you wanted,
a crop duster's yellow plane
diving so low
the weeds shimmied,
you floating down,
in no hurry
at last, to the earth
you claimed
always knew you
better than
you knew yourself.

Blackberry Road

Piney woods
where we played Fort Apache
oozed rosin.

Cow pies baked
in the dog day

heat while we picked
what our Mama
had promised she'd turn

into cobblers
come supper time.

Braving those
thorny hells, we risked an arm.
Then a leg. Half a torso

till trapped
we stood stubborn as martyrs

awhile before
we pulled our mortal flesh free,
praying hard

not to spill what
we'd gathered.

By then it was noon
and so hot we lost faith
and walked home,

scratching bug-bites
and snag-wounds,

displaying our blackberries
   domed in the pot
     the way church deacons hoisted

     collection plates
while we sang "Gloria Patri."

The gnats smelled us coming
   and haloed our heads
     when we reached the backyard

     where splayed in the cool dirt
they'd dug under lantana bushes

     our daddy's hounds
snored like the back pews each Sunday
     before Benediction.

First Presbyterian

Sitting in church every Sunday, I hated the hats
I had to wear. They were small things with net
attached. Or hard plastic fruit. They did not fit
and sometimes they fell into the aisle or my lap
if my mother had not pierced their velveteen
skins with hat pins she wove through my stiff
hair-sprayed hair. There was no way to scratch

my small soul through those hats. No way
I could sit through the sermons if not daydreaming
out of them, using the blank wall beside the piano
as movie screen, imagining myself hatless, free
of my hair spray and beehive, my hair grown
miraculously long, trailing hat pins across
the small town, heading north toward what soon

would be interstate. What happened next?
Let us pray, said the preacher and I came awake,
though I shut my eyes dutifully. What was
he saying that I should heed, who was this God
who knew everything? Why should I pull on a girdle
and hose for His sake and sit waiting for Him
to call? *Just As I Am*, we sang, closing the service.
My soul took a deep breath and walked out.

Some Rock Remembers

Rocks want to be noticed. Just ask the one
webbed with lichen that brought me down
onto the banks of Ramsey Cascades. She
knew what she was doing. She and her sisters
sang all afternoon while I lay

with my ankle in fragments and waited
for rescue. The song they sang? I'm still
trying to learn it. The first words go something
like this: *Here, here, here.* Or was it
Now, now, now? For three hours I listened.
Most days I never remember their song.
I walk as I ever did on my anklebones

knitted together, a patchwork as precious
as any quilt thrown on a bed for a cold body
needing the stitchery of *Double Wedding Ring*
or *Hands All Around.* The pattern
my knitted bones make I name *Some Rock
Remembers.* Our body-to-body encounter.
First impression so sudden that I could do nothing
but scream. The rock? She kept her cool.

Big Tease

Little by little, the earth sheds
her veils. Lets her white blossoms
tremble. The river shakes out her blue

shimmy and scrubs it to smithereens
over the singing rocks, leaving her
sunny side up, such a tease
that I sway to her music

as if I am Salome's sister,
and not an old woman who knows
that the inkblot of sky on this page
of my daybook will soon begin fading,

because how can anyone, even Great
Granddaddy Death, stay asleep
amid so much awakening?

Night Fishing

I bait my lines
with the scent of old planks
rotting over the muddy Flint
River where drowsy snakes
coil in the rushes and lightning
bugs fizzle like spirits
of night crawlers nibbled
by minnows. No catch
in my throat but this aching
to wade into lazy black water
and stand all night long
in its leave-taking, calling
the fish home to Mama.

Glorified

Whenever I praise what she's brought forth,
whether biscuits or chicken stewed all day
with sweet corn and gumbo, she answers, *To God
Be the Glory.* I tell her I don't mess around
with an old man who's so far away he can't hear me.
I'd rather be talking to petunias that bloom on her porch,
or the bathrobe she wears when she's making
the coffee, her toes while she's sleeping in front
of the t.v., her big mouth that's snoring.
To you be the Glory, I say, feeling
so brazen this morning, I dare God
to give me the finger. "Go scrub out
your mouth," she scolds, but I see her smiling.

Thinking Myself Home

I have to look up and over the trees
all the way to the mountains I see in the distance,

then hang a left soon as I get there,
thinking my way down the Blue Ridge

and into the piedmont just south
of Atlanta. From there it's a straight

shoot to home,
if I still want to go, which I do

because this is the best way,
by stealth, no one knows I am coming,

no cake to be baked,
and my mother not worrying most of her day

by the telephone, clearly imagining
fifty-car pileups,

the ambulance wailing, the whole bloody
nine miles of interstate closed

for the body count.
No idle comments about my new haircut,

my extra pounds. I could be dust
on the air or a bright stab of light passing through.

I don't have to stay long.
I can leave when I want to, without feeling guilty

when I see my father's eyes squinching
back tears as I drive away.

Hello and goodbye. That's it.
And I'm back

in my bedroom that faces south into the side
of these trees, with the radio on

warning Traveler's Advisory. Wrecking-ball hailstones.
King Kong tornado. Megaton Blizzard.

A forecast so unimaginably bad, only a fool
would drive home in this kind of weather.

Beginning at the Bottom

the bottom of the backwoods . . .

—*THE ATLANTA JOURNAL-CONSTITUTION*, DESCRIBING
MY HOME COUNTY IN THE 1950S

My small-town backwater library,
behind the bank,
across from the post office,
floats to the surface of right now,

daylight drifting through window
shades onto the wooden floor,
golden light, let's call it,
because to say *sepia* places

it into a scrapbook, and this story
still lives inside the folds
of my mind's aging labyrinth,
its infinite pages bound

fast in their signatures,
spines named and numbered,
its nooks where I hid myself,
lifting a book to my nostrils,

as if I could sniff out
a good story, just like my grandfather's
bird-dogs flushed quail
from the underbrush. Sometimes

I heard whispers rise
from a neighboring bookshelf,
a telephone ringing, the bookmobile
laboring home from the backwoods

and always the light bulbs
in every lamp humming like bees
round a sweet pool of soda spilled
onto the pavement.

To that hive of bookshelves,
I journey again,
letting go of my one life
to enter the stories of others,

still hungry for words
and the way they can bring me back
home to my senses,
the way they reach out to the world.

Easter Afternoon

All morning we'd climbed until
we reached a primitive graveyard
whose stones bore no names we could read.
The season too early for wildflowers,
we searched for other unfoldings,
cumulus climbing the afternoon's
trellises. Branch water cascading.

Creek side, we nibbled the chocolate
eggs filled with marshmallow cream
we had bought on a whim
from a shelf bare of all but a few baskets
no child had wanted this year
or the last, no expiration date
stamped on their green wrappings.

Not like the hard-boiled eggs in their nest
of cellophane grass I shoved under my bed.
They decomposed like the flesh I heard preachers
declare doomed, yet saved by the sun
rising over an empty tomb.

Through tiny holes, my aunts blew
the yolks from their eggs
to craft miniature worlds within
empty shells. I marveled at how they made
something so fragile hold fast.
Swans adrift on an emerald pond. A bride
in her almost invisible veil.
How long would those eggs last
displayed on a shelf? Kept under glass?

Easter sky. Another one. Blue
as an egg being raised from its dye cup.
Upon it the script left behind
by a passing jet. A spiral
of buzzards adrift on a thermal,
the blades of their wings
sudden gold as the sun sets.

LAST LIGHT

The tests I need to pass are prescribed by the spirits
of place who understand travel but not amnesia.
—FROM "THIS IS MY THIRD AND LAST ADDRESS
    TO YOU," ADRIENNE RICH

1.

Almost the age when memory falters,
I fear being made to count backward
by seven's, to answer to date, year, and
presidents, as if those numbers and names
matter more in the end than this place
where I stand at the same kitchen window,
observing the same pines set swaying by wind,
reaching upward as I'll reach, come morning,
my arms to the ceiling, breathing the dark out
of body and spirit, exhaling that old dream
of nothingness: laying my head down to sleep.

2.

Now Rocky Face Ridge catches fire
in the last light and, though I can't hear it
from where I stand, Cullowhee Creek tumbles into
the Tuckaseegee, always unscrolling beneath me
the names I already know. Snowbird.
Buzzards Roost. Weyahutta. Oconaluftee.

3.

I don't know how long names can last
if there's no one to care where they live.
What I saw on the hairpin curve down from
the Chimney Tops, white as snow, I've not forgotten.
Phacelia. And how, on the trail leading

up to the summit of Sunkota Ridge,
I saw sauntering toward me a young woman
I could have sworn was the reincarnation of
every spring wildflower ever named anywhere.

4.

Closer she comes to me each April,
as if she means more than I have a lifetime
to know. Roundabout her, her white Easter dress
whispers every thing I want to keep living
here in this valley that cups the last swallow of light,
every name I must reach to remember or else
lose them, hillside by hillside, to darkness.

Here

From the southernmost reaches of night,
I have come here to stand at this window. Here I can see
    winter trees line dancing on the horizon and glimpse over traffic
        the bolt of the gray Tuckaseegee
        unrolling its sackcloth.

No ashes, just a rusty gate I jimmied
        open at evensong
    onto an arcade of pecan trees,
    rows merging into the unseen, the underside,
through which I've followed a lacework of trails
    to their jump-offs, where sky always waits
    like an ocean in which I hear voices roll over me.

No wonder, leaving my father's black fields,
        where the dirt smelled of duty and death
        and the sunset burned all the way down to its roots
            and let wildfire leap over
            the ditches and burn up the sky,
I arrived, not a moment too soon, at the junction
    of Thomas Divide and Kanati Fork,
    air ripe with bear scat and leaf mold.

Or was it because of the windows where every night I watched
    the sky field on fire dying out, cloud by cloud,
            into darkness, that I came
to this place where sky huddles over the Balsams
        and lingers awhile every morning
as mist lifting off the weeds clasping the edges of Cullowhee
        Creek? Over thirty years I've watched the way
light begins here. It still wakes me up. Lets me be.
        Here. Where I am.